D1500909

6th Grade Middle School Chronicles

Where NO Secrets Are Kept

Written by
Essynce E. Moore

6th Grade Middle School Chronicles

Copyright © 2015 by Starr M. Barrett

Essynce Couture Publishing

P.O. Box 5082

Hillside, NJ 07205

Printed in the United States of America
Published by Essynce Couture Publishing
Hillside, NJ 07205
Editor: Essynce Couture Publishing
Cover Photos: Evan Whitney
Cover Design: Jamar Hargrove - Owner of NeedGFX.com
Essynce E. Moore
Entrepreneur, Motivational Speaker, Actress, Author, Fashion Designer & Stylist, Founder and CEO of Essynce Couture, LLC. and Essynce Couture University (ECU)
www.essyncecouture.com

ISBN-13: 978-0692392362)

Printed in USA by Essynce Couture Publishing

I dedicate this book to
all Middle School survivors.
Thank You!

6th Grade Middle School Chronicles

Table of Contents:

Introduction

Essynce E. Moore

Introduction:

80% of people look at age before personality. In 6th grade age is the last thing that matters. I mean, we have kissing, hugging, dating and more from people you thought you knew. I mean, what the "fryck" is going on?!?

Fryck, my world's famous word, meaning: "a bitter-sweet, trendy expression."
WARNING!!! I will be saying this a lot!!!

Now, where was I? As a fashion designer balancing homework and clothes...things can get quite complicated. Also, while reading this you'll see me lose and gain some friends, but I guess that's the way life is. Middle School though... is a new story and I don't remember signing up for Degrassi Reality. #lol

Chapter 1: Then & Now

Chapter 1

Then & Now

<u>Monday</u>

So here's the deal at the moment it's second semester so I'm going to jump from my first day of school to well... now. My first day of middle school started off with me putting on my burgundy and gray uniform. I wore a knee-length skirt and a burgundy top. Man, do I hate uniforms!

When I got to school, I walked in the building and greeted friends who I hadn't seen in forever. I met my teachers who were either cool, nice or strict. Some were too nice if you know what I mean. Tbh: (To Be Honest) it was my first time having to move and walk through the building to get to another class. I ended up walking into so many of the WRONG classrooms and I was just lost! I almost cried because of how lost I was. That sucked!!

<u>Tuesday</u>

Alright so that was then and well it's now. Let me introduce you to my friends. There's Amy, my best friend since kindergarten. She's crazy, fun, yells a lot and tends to say "fryck" (Fryck – a bitter/sweet trendy expression) a lot like me. I've got a lot of my friends saying that now.

Next, there's Sofia. I guess you can say she's Instagram crazy. She's always saying how Essynce Couture has a lot of followers, but not a lot of likes and how my personal Instagram page has not a lot of followers, but a "decent" amount of likes. I mean, like dude COME ON!! Plus she tends to ask a whole lot of stupid questions. Once she asked me "what would I do if my mom called me ugly?" Tbh: I replied, "Questions like that aggravate me." Even though she does all of these things she's still my friend. Hopefully we won't become frenemies.

I already have one of those and her name is CeCe. Cece's a friend and an enemy, therefore she's a frenemy. I'll give her props though. She's not as annoying as she used to be. CeCe is the kind of person to go out with to birthday sleepovers, waterparks and skating. But when you want someone to support you or help you with something, that's not where you want to go. That's where having Amy as a best friend can be helpful.

Next, before you start thinking this is an all-girls book, one of my best friend's is also a "guy" named Chris. Now here's the thing about Chris: He's cool but very sensitive. In other words, he takes things a little too personally. Like today when he kind of got a little angry when he lost some basketball competition thing we did in gym class.

But I appreciate that Chris definitely likes to be involved with Essynce Couture. He's like my brother. Alright, so next is Alice, who's ghetto and proud. Alice is definitely my sister though. She's really pretty. Alice, out of everyone in our little crew, is closest to Alex who you'll meet soon. Alice is more afraid to look a mess than get in a fight. I don't even thing she cares if she gets in a fight. She's cool like that. Hanging out with her will definitely make you laugh and be interested in what she has to say next. Even though she's all of these things, you can still catch her in class taking notes and being focused. Well, almost focused. ;-)

After introducing Alice, I'm going to introduce my other best "guy" friend, Zack. Alright, if you know Zack, you know you're gonna laugh and that's how I'm going to start off this little intro on him. He purposely tries to bug me by calling Essynce Couture "Essynce Culture". But I wouldn't know what I'd do without him. He's my bro. Also he told me he has my back and he always does. Sometimes (more like always) I'll be carrying a lot of books in the hall and he'll help me out. Note to all boys: Girls do appreciate when you do that.

Okay, next is Lizzy. Now before we start, here's the thing about her: She's always "dug" Chris, if you know what I mean. They've went out, he dumped her, they went out again, he cheated on her and she stayed with him till he dumped her AGAIN! Basically, the process continues, but Chris doesn't cheat anymore and I think Lizzy only dumped him like once. I'm sure they're gonna go out again next year.

Okay, in real life I have a little pet name for Lizzy that I'm not going to mention because her identity remains a mystery. But really I love Lizzy. She's like my sister. It's weird because we started off not liking each other back in the 5th grade.

Last for now but definitely not least – and I mentioned her a little earlier – is Alex. One thing I love about Alex is her hugs. They're so warm and cozy. Alex is definitely a cool tomboy who you kind of relate to as soon as you start a conversation with her. She's a lot like Alice and she tends to rock box-braids. **Don't worry I have more friends who we'll meet along the way.**

Notes:

_____

_____

_____

_____

_____

_____

_____

_____

Chapter 2:
We R The Crazy Kids!!!

Chapter 2

We R The Crazy Kids!!!

<u>Wednesday</u>

Okay so I'm already ticked off because I got a detention for being late. That's messed up... I mean, since when do you know what people go through at home to give them a detention for being late. Seriously, judge much?! Tbh: I'm not only angry. I'm upset. I don't like getting detention. I know I'm a good kid. I just don't think I deserve it.

Okay so besides that this is a pretty decent day. But I'm stressed out. Report cards come out next week and my grade for library dropped from a B to a C. Yeah it doesn't seem like a big deal, but a C can hold me back from honor roll, and I ALWAYS make honor roll. I've made it every year. It's definitely recurring goal. At the moment, I'm in Mr. Cooper's class, where everyone claims he can't handle the workload. I think he's too nice. Everyone walks all over him and honestly I feel bad.

It isn't just his fault. It's some of the kids' fault too. They are the CRAZY kids. I mean we only spend 20 minutes out of about two hours learning.

Thursday

Alrighty, so the rest of Wednesday was a pretty normal day. Nothing big (learn, learn, learn, learn) so I'm taking you to Thursday. Mr. Cooper was absent today, so we had a substitute. When I hear "substitute," I think, "Yeah, no homework!!!" Plus, I had Ms. T before and she's pretty cool. But today I think my perspective on her changed. She gave us the worksheets our teacher left for us and told us that we could whisper to each other. I think we've all had that "whisper" teacher. So, I'm doing the work ...everyone's talking and then BAM! I hit problem number 7, page 2. I don't understand it! Since we can whisper I walked over to my friend Lilly, to see if she can help. Don't worry. Lilly's a good, quiet, and smart kid in Mr. Cooper's class, which is a hard kid to find. I walked over to Lilly and since we sit in desks that are connected to the chairs I asked her to scoot over. Lilly and I are cool, so she did. We're discussing the problem that's complicated for both of us and Ms. T, from the back of the room yells "Hey, what's wrong with you ...why are you sitting on her?"

Lilly and I turned around to find Ms. T is looking at us. I had a confused look on my face and so did Lilly. Then I finally yelled," I'm not sitting on her." That was the weirdest thing I'd said all day. I also manage to tell her that I just needed help.

Ms. T must have seen a weird angle of me that made it look like I was sitting on Lilly, but I wasn't. Also, she must of not heard me because after I told her I just needed help she said, "That's no reason to sit on her. Go to your seat." As angry and confused as I was, I went to my seat, still lost about the problem. Thank goodness the bell rang a while after.

Oh and I almost forgot to tell you the security guards had to come in to take out the bad kids. It was a normal day because of that. They came in every week. Today, I had Social Studies, Gym, Language Arts, Computers, and my favorite: LUNCH! At the moment, I'm at this detention I mentioned earlier for being late and... It's A Blast!

We get to play games, eat ice cream, and... April Fools! Oh my, BaD ...I forgot to tell you it's April 1st, aka (also known as) April Fools. Really, what we're doing is...NOTHING!! 44 minutes of nothing. Well the other kids aren't, I'm just here in the school's auditorium writing and telling you guys how I frycken feel. Which really isn't that bad. I'm a little surprised about that myself. I mean, when I first got the detention, well...I looked like this :-\ but I felt like this :-0 (surprised), :-((angry), ;'((sad). I guess we all feel those things, but we have to manage to keep that blank face :-\, especially in middle school.

Notes:

_____

_____

_____

_____

_____

_____

_____

_____

_____

Chapter 3:
Two Much on my Mind

Chapter 3
Two Much on my Mind

Today my friend's and I, who are both in Mr. Cooper's class, were discussing what we're gonna do for the NJ Ask. The NJ Ask is the test at the end of the year here in New Jersey that determines whether we pass to the next grade or not. It also determines the classes we'll have next year. That's why this year I'm in honors Language Arts. I'm a really good writer and I really like to do it. In fact, writing poetry in particular was going to be my "back bone," if my careers in acting, designing, and dancing don't work out. But that's a different story. Let's go back to middle school.

Alice, Mia and I…(Mia: my friend, smart, cool, crazy) were thinking when we take the math section of the NJ Ask we aren't going to be able to focus in Mr. Cooper's class with those kids or as I call them "animals." We were thinking maybe we can take the test in our school library or maybe the principal's office. Mr. Parker, our principal, knows what goes on the classroom…CHAOS!!

At the moment, I'm in Ms. A's class. She's strict, but still one of my favorite teachers. Favorite Teacher List:

1. ~~~~~~~

2. Ms. A (You Rock!!)

3. ~~~~~~~

4. ~~~~~~~

5. ~~~~~~~

A few kids call her mean, but I call her fair. It's sometimes hard for people to see the difference between the two. Ms. A is checking our homework right now and she has us passing around some of our class work to each other to look at it, I guess. All I'm thinking about is the bell…after it rings, it's lunch. Mmmmmmm… lunch sounds so good right now. I'm so hungry and I know I'm getting a little off topic, but I just want to clarify something and that something is I'd never say I'm so "thirsty" in from of these kids. They'll take it COMPLETELY the wrong way. Oooohhh….

Now back on topic…

Ms. A gave the class after-school detention because some of the kids were talking. The main reason I'm upset about that is because it's my dad's birthday and I planned on spending some after school time with him.

Luckily, by the end of the class some of the kids helped each other get their things together and because of that Ms. A let us off the hook. My mom packed me lunch today, which I very much prefer. The lunch at school is okay, I guess…but I trust food from my own house a bit more. What do you prefer? Since after I ate my lunch I've been chewing on this gum I got that is so good. It's Sour Patch Kids flavored and I love it. Now, don't worry I don't chew it in class…well at least not all the time. I usually chew it around the end of lunch and outside for "recess" afterwards.

Oh and I forgot to tell you at lunch today a kid also named Chris (NOT the one I told you about earlier) got in a fight at lunch. The fight occurred in the lunch line. Of course, one of the security guards went to break it up, but when Chris tried to fight the security to get back to the other kid he was fighting, the security guard pinned him DOWN!!! It almost looked like he was choking him, good thing he wasn't.

So, this week is the last week of school before Spring Break . I don't usually do a lot for spring break, but since my mom is taking off work for the week I know we have some fun things planned. My only problem with Spring Break is the fact that sadly some of my teachers don't understand the "break" part of Spring Break. I love my …well SOME of my teachers, but I don't want any frycken Spring Break packet! I have a Math, Language Arts and Social Studies packet.

They're all graded!! Huhhhhh…give me a break. I mean I give you months and months of my focus and time. I'm just trying to cherish this one week. Plus, the NJ Ask is in just two weeks. There's enough pressure already there. The only thing I like about the NJ Ask is it's a week with no classes and, best of all, NO HOMEWORK!!

I've been thinking a lot about what to expect for the test because I'm trying to get all the thoughts out early so they don't bug me during break.

Notes:

_____

_____

_____

_____

_____

_____

_____

_____

Chapter 4: NJ Ask +

Chapter 4

NJ Ask +

This week for the NJ Ask, my back has finally gotten a break. In other words, for this whole week I don't need to bring my book bag to school. That's a giant relief for me because my back usually is really sore by the time I get home from school. I always have a lot of homework and books needed to do it.

My book bag consists of:

-4 Notebooks

-1 Pencil Case

-An occasional Social Studies (S.S.) book

-A Multi-Folder

-My Glasses

-Phone

-House Key

-Headphones (in case I ever have to walk home)

-A book for Language Arts

-Agenda

-Wallet

-And more

See what homework and work does to us teachers? Physical pain. Just kidding…maybe.

For the state test (NJ Ask) each section is divided into four parts. Monday and Tuesday is Language Arts. Wednesday and Thursday is Math. Friday's Science, but I'm in the 6th grade and I don't need to worry about that. That's only for 8th graders.

Our testing schedule is…first do part 1 of that section. Then do part 2 for that same section. In between parts 2 and 3 we take a bathroom break and stretch. I cherish the heck out of that break. The test is pretty stressful. After part 3 we go to lunch. Later, after lunch, if we brought games or something we can play them in the classroom. Oh and I almost forgot to tell you during the test Mr. Cooper wasn't there and we had two teachers come to…basically watch us, I guess. Their names are Ms. Ellen and Mr. Edward. They would give us our test, give us our #2 pencils and read us the directions.

Ms. Ellen was really good with the class and sometimes after lunch she took us outside to the jungle gym. It was really fun! Usually, after lunch I'd bring this game called Mancala and I taught some of my friends how to play it. Everyone became obsessed with playing. I constantly heard things such as, "Essynce, can I play… Essynce, I'm next right…Hey, I was here first, tell them Essynce." It was pretty annoying, but I still brought the game. It's really fun!

Around Thursday, after lunch, around the end of the day, I told my friend Lilly…Lilly (quiet, sweet, open, no secrets)…to research something when she got home and to keep it a secret.

She said she wouldn't tell anymore but the minute I turned around she went on my friend Bea's (Sweet, Popular, Funny) phone and looked it up. Then when I realized how awkwardly quiet it got behind me, I turned around and saw Bea on her phone reading word for word what I asked Lilly to research. Don't worry I only asked her to research something about Sponge-Bob, but I was still angry that she couldn't keep the secret.

I mean, dude, are you frycken serious? Though what really made me mad is when I turned around and before Bea even read aloud the search I asked "What's going on?" Lilly replied by saying, "Nothing." She said nothing as if she did nothing. I did feel a little bad for her though because as soon as she saw I was mad she put her head on her desk as if she was about to cry.

Eventually – also known as two days later, not including the weekend I forgave her. Now, we're talking as if nothing ever happened. Though on Friday, I didn't go to school. It was "Bring your Child to Work Day" so I went to see my mom's work/job. One week later after the test, everything was partly back to usual. By partly, I mean a lot of the kids have "turn't up" because since the test is over they feel that the school year is over. That's why I think the NJ Ask should be towards the end of the year. What do you think? Also, Mr. Cooper's back but I miss, Ms. Ellen. She understood us not only as students but as kids/people. I appreciated that. You don't find these types of teachers every day.

Notes:

_____

_____

_____

_____

_____

_____

_____

_____

_____

Chapter 5: Keeping My Cool

Chapter 5

Keeping Me Cool

Today my mom told me before I went to school that I only have two more months. Anytime a teacher gets on my nerves I just keep repeating that to myself to keep my cool. I'm not the snap-on-a-teacher and get-suspended type.

Today my classmates and I were locked out of Mr. Cooper's class, the lights were off and everything. For about three minutes we sat down on the hall floor asking each other what the heck was going on. Finally I got up and headed towards the front of the school, where I saw one of the security guards. After I explained to him the reason for my being in the front of the school, he directed me towards the main office, in a bit of a disrespectful tone. Only two more months Essynce. Keep your cool, I thought to myself. In the main office, I was directed towards another office not too far away.

By then, I'd repeated the same story three times. "My classmates and I are locked out of the classroom, and the lights are off so I don't think our teacher is in there." In the office I was informed that there was one substitute who hadn't showed up yet and the women behind the desk also suggested that I notify my classmates about the new piece of information. I mumbled a polite "thank you" and made my way out of the classroom. Walking back to my classroom I saw Mr. Tom, my music teacher, and I shot him a quick "Hi." He's a cool teacher and he responded by shooting me back a "What's up Essynce?"

When I got back to the outside of the classroom I sat back down on the floor and soon realized that the twist in my hair was coming out. I went to my locker, which was only a few centimeters away, because I had a mirror inside and that's when I found…it. A disgusting glob of gum stuck to the front of my locker like a magnet stuck to iron. I asked Lilly, who was next to me for a piece of paper and then I used it to peel the gum off. After a while of talking, sitting and a bit of eating, the substitute finally showed up. The tall, middle-aged woman unlocked the classroom door, signaling for most of us to stand up and prepare for the day. Lilly and I stood up, off the floor against some of the lockers, ready to enter the classroom.

I was holding my binder and text book in my arms, when some overly done makeup wearing diva came by and pushed me out the way to get through my classmates and I. Honestly, if I would have heard a simple "excuse me" come out her mouth I would have easily moved but I didn't hear it and believe me when I say I am not going to stop-drop-and-roll for some local 8th grader. As she walked away her sidekick kept peeking back at Lilly and I. When they were finally out of sight Lilly and I glanced at each other while smiling. With our unscientifically proven telepathic bond we both knew what the other was thinking and we ended up busting out laughing at the fact that this girl pushed me and she's mad. Like, dude, you pushed me! You were the one who made the physical contact! So why are YOU the mad one? Huhh…this is too much for 8 o'clock in the morning. Shortly after that Mean Girls scenario we all entered the classroom. The substitute was a woman most of the class, including me, was already familiar with. I recognized her as the woman who came in every so often to help Mr. Cooper out with the class. One of the guys in the classroom respectfully asked our substitute, Ms. F, if she was our substitute for the day. Ms. F rudely responded by saying, "I'm not a substitute. I am a certified teacher who teaches teachers how to be teachers." Pretend I said that in a slightly mocking tone because even if this lady was a blah blah blah who teaches blah blah blah, she wasn't our teacher. Therefore, making her a substitute. Now I'm not usually like this. I'll usually mind my own business, but I don't like this substitute.

She always finds some way to accuse me of something, like that cliché teacher in the movies who is always out to get that one kid…that one, poor kid. Unfortunately, in my story I'm that kid. For example, today a girl in my classroom asked me what today's date was and I must have turned into Junior from Problem Child because Ms. F put me on blast, yelling at me for saying, and I quote, "The 19th." Apparently, we're not supposed to be talking during a game of BINGO!!! As much as I wanted to yell in Ms. F's face I turned to the board with a big grin plastered on my face and said aloud those three words that were allowing me to hold on to my sanity. "Two more months." Only two more months of school. Only two more months of school. Alice, who was sitting next to me looked at me and started laughing.

I guess she knew I was hanging on by the skin of my teeth before erupting like a volcano. Also I probably looked insane with that big grin because I obviously wasn't happy. Alice always said she wanted to see that side of me, the side where no limits are tolerated and what WANTS to be said GETS said. No hesitation or reluctance whatsoever. Did I forget to mention that we were playing homemade bingo? Yeah you read correctly. Homemade bingo. We legitimately ripped out pieces of scrap papers from our notebooks and wrote down random numbers, with the letters B.I.N.G.O written above all the numbers at the very top of the paper. The caller simply called out any number his heart desired. This was bootleg bingo. Anyway, Alice got bingo and her prize was a homemade chocolate chip cookie that Ms. F made herself. Alice also got to be caller for the next round. Now I know what you're probably thinking, "Essynce even if you don't like Ms. F you know you wanted that cookie." Well guess what I didn't. I don't like chocolate...sue me.

Notes:

_____

_____

_____

_____

_____

_____

_____

_____

_____

Chapter 6: Five Days a Week

Chapter 6

Five Days a Week

If you can survive a week in my school then you can survive the Civil War, point blank. No hesitation or excuses, believe me you will survive. With all the chaotic events that occurred, this week in particular, I think some of us students can survive a World War III. But before we get ahead of ourselves let's take this week from the top, starting off on Monday.

Monday

Recently, my friend Briana-

Briana-popular, funny, cute

was caught in basically a 6th grade love triangle. Let's just say the boys in my school love the idea of dating her. Anyway, the triangle consist of…

Joe-Popular, funny, player

Jimmy-New in our school, nice, pretty eyes

And of course Briana.

Later that very Monday Briana told me how both guys asked her out…through text message. Why am I not surprised? Briana showed me both conversations and they were complete opposites. Joe flirted more and tried to use his "charm" that I found quite amusing, while Jimmy was more personal and explained every detail as to why he wanted Briana to go out with him. Briana also mentioned how Jimmy wrote her a paragraph, explaining once again, why he liked her. I'll admit saying all of that takes guts, simply being able to say hi to your crush takes guts, so I have to give both guys props.

<u>Tuesday</u>

Now today not much happened, except for the detention selfie. The kids once again got detention a second time in Ms. A's class for talking. By 3:15 p.m. – "aka" when I get out of school – my classmates and I met up with each other in the auditorium. But before I went back in the school I pulled out my phone and called my mom to let her know we had detention.

That particular day she was picking me up. In the auditorium Ms. A wasn't there yet so Briana, Zack, and some of my other friends sat on the chairs talking. Then Briana comes up with the idea that we all take a selfie, so she pulled out her Samsung S3 phone and we all took a selfie. I decided to do the same thing so out popped my Samsung S5 and we took two selfies together. When Ms. A came, we all got quiet and she said how we're only going to be there for about five minutes. It was a pretty normal detention, we just sat there quietly. By the time Ms. A dismissed us I showed her our selfies.

She took my phone with a grin on her face, stopped one of my other teacher's, Mr. Snooze and waved my phone in his face saying, "This is what they do in detention." We all started laughing and I was handed my phone back. I waved good-bye and left.

Wednesday

On Wednesday a few small but interesting things happened in Mr. Cooper's class. For one thing Alice wore this black vest to school and it had fur on the hoodie. (We're not allowed to wear hoodies to school.) Chris asked if he could see it and he put it on. I kept telling him to take it off because it looked…WRONG, but he didn't listen until the end of class.

Also, later on that same day one of my friends who I will not say the name of said that once Mr. Cooper wouldn't let them use the bathroom. In our school we need the teachers to sign our passes for the hall to go to places like the bathroom, the water fountain, etc. So this particular friend ended up forging Mr. Cooper's signature and left anyway. Everyone says his signature is super easy to master and I don't want to be the guilty student to find out.

Thursday

On Thursday, I had a violin concert. I've played violin since I was about 9, in the 4th grade. Anyway, at the concert I decided to shoot a "Fashion Fryck" video. Fashion Fryck is the Essynce Couture web show I do for my clothing line. A while back my mom and I teamed up with her friend "Uncle Magic" to start creating Fashion Fryck shows. Although things didn't work out with Uncle Magic, I continued to do my web shows since I loved doing them. To sum it up the web shows are about all things fashion.

41

So when I was preparing to shoot I made sure I asked my school's principal first for permission. I asked my vice principal and he kindly directed me to Mr. Parker, the head principal. He also was my principal for the 4th grade. I explained to Mr. Parker how I shoot Fashion Fryck videos and he said okay, as long as I don't mention the schools name or anything. I interviewed my friends about what they were wearing and stuff... It was pretty fun! It also is still on my YouTube channel, which is Essynce Moore. I named the video "Behind the Scenes - at my violin concert." It turned out pretty good once I edited the lighting, added music and other revisions.

Friday

On Friday, three of my friend's got injured and the funny thing is I bet you they "turn't up" over the weekend anyway.

On that Friday morning in Mr. Cooper's class, Chris got into a yelling argument with this girl named Tea. We were in the same class last year, but I don't know her enough to know what their argument was about. But, I do know that Tea took a blade and threw it at Chris's back. By blade I don't mean a knife or anything. I mean a rectangular metal object, with really sharp ends. I'm sure it hurt Chris a little, I could tell though by the angle that she threw the blade that it couldn't hurt possibly as bad as Chris made it seem. I mean, the way he acted you'd think he had been shot. Chris even had Mr. Cooper carry his stuff for him. Tea ended up getting reported and I think she got suspended for a couple of days. Later on that Friday after lunch, Amy, Alex, Alice and I went outside for recess.

Oh and this girl, Ciara, who's hung out with us for a while went too. When we got outside it was pretty warm. We all just walked around and talked for a bit. Alice and Ciara ended up playing and Alice, being light, hopped on Ciara's back. Ciara held on to Alice's legs and went running to scare Alice.

They both ended up falling on one of the thick roots coming up from the ground from the nearby tree. They both laughed it off, but Alice cut her knee which was bleeding and Ciara cut the side of her stomach which was also bleeding. I thought it was kind of weird because although their scratches were in different places they looked so similar. Ciara's looked a bit more serious though.

Amy and I went to one of the teacher's outside and we asked if we could help the girls inside to the nurse's office. Amy took Ciara's book bag and walked her in and I took Alice's book bag and walked her in. Alice traded off putting her arm around Amy and I because her leg hurt and she needed some help walking. Don't get all emotional though because ALL of us laughed about their fall on the way in.

Notes:

_____

_____

_____

_____

_____

_____

_____

_____

_____

Chapter 7: Growth

Chapter 7

Growth

Recently saying only two more months of school just jumped to two weeks and three half days. My emotions for some of my teachers have grown and most aren't in a pleasing way.

Let's start off with Mr. Snooze. Today we were working on a project involving cockroaches. He passed out two in each container. We were going to observe them in class that day. The two kids at my table and I looked at them with a feeling of interest, though I was a bit...DISGUSTED, to be honest. Anyway, Mr. Snooze explained the rules like: no talking loudly while they're out and stuff like that, and then I realized how much he cared about these insects. I whispered to one of the kids next to me that I wish we got that kind of sympathy when we got homework or tests. Then I thought about how at least his work isn't all that hard. Eventually, when all the containers were passed out there was one group who still didn't have anything, so out of all the groups Mr. Snooze came to ours and took one of the cockroaches away. I begged him not to because I was quite fascinated.

I didn't become angry till Mr. Snooze rudely in a voice that was not yelling but was "hardcore" and unsympathetic said, "Deal with It!" At that moment there were so many harsh things I wanted to say, as the words repeated in my head over and over again. "Deal with it...deal with it...deal with it!" But I knew I hadn't been raised to go off on a teacher, so I just worked with the one cockroach we had and pretended I hadn't heard a thing.

Okay, so recently one of my favorite teachers, Mr. Tim, had a bit of a problem with our class and for a while some of my classmates and I were mad at him too, which isn't usual. Okay, so this conflict began on Friday. Our school was trying something new so our class schedules were a bit different. Our 3rd block which, if you don't know, is two periods combined – had been cut in half and the 6th graders lunch was squeezed in between.

It's basically like a sandwich:

- **Period**
- **Lunch**   **=**   **1 Block**
- **Period**

In the first part of 3rd block, Mr. Tim explained to us how he was going to be absent for 2nd period because he was going to take the 7th graders to field day. Field day, in my district, is when a specific grade of kids go to a park or field and do all kinds of obstacles or activities with their classmates and sometimes it will lead up to a prize.

I personally liked field day more in 2nd grade when there were water balloon fights and stuff like that. Anyway, Mr. Tim said how he wasn't going to be there when we got back and we needed to read the book for the marking period and answer some questions.

When we got back from lunch Mr. Tim wasn't there, there was a substitute. I saw how some of my friends started working on the questions, so I went to join them. About five minutes before the bell rang, kids just began to notice on the board there was a note left from Mr. Tim.

It read:
Remember when you're finished reading to do the assignment left on my desk…it counts as a quiz grade.

WHAT?!? Neither the substitute nor Mr. Tim mentioned an assignment that counts as a quiz grade. My friends and I rushed to Mr. Tim's desk and noticed how on the sheet we were paired into groups; we had a choice for each of us to pick an individual part of the project. On that sheet it said how if any of us were absent we'd just cancel out that particular job. I knew that we would not have enough time so I thought over the weekend would I just cancel out all the jobs that aren't mine?

I thought the same thing as everyone else; that Mr. Tim would understand and let us do the assignment on Monday, when we see him next. Instead, on Monday he became furious! He even doubled the quiz grade on purpose so all of our grades would drop. He assumed that while he was gone all we did was fool around and talk. That wasn't true!! The reading just took more time.

My mom emailed Mr. Tim and he explained that we have another assignment that should boost up our grades. Mia was still mad though because her grade dropped BIG TIME! Eventually, I boosted my grade up to a decent B, but Mia was still mad that Mr. Tim never changed our grades back in the first place.

Next, Mr. Cooper's been bugging me. I went to feeling pity for him because he couldn't handle the class disliking him and being disrespectful. I don't even think my mom likes him as a teacher. Anyway, I think the big change started when he started pulling me out individually and thinking that I had that kind of relationship to joke around with him.

Example 1:
Pulling me out individually.

Recently, since the school year's coming to an end, Mr. Cooper's been letting us get away with sitting where we want, so once I was working on a sheet he gave us and it was hard. I knew I needed help and Mia and I work well together, so I got up and we shared her desk chair to go over the problems. Then the situation started when Mr. Cooper said, "Essynce, can you go back to your seat?" See, I would have been okay with it; I could have easily gone back to my seat, but when I looked up I saw kids walking around, standing, talking and Tea was even sitting on TOP of a desk.

I looked at Mr. Cooper with a confused look on my face. I thought what makes me stand out so much out of all these kids that I need to go to my seat? I looked at Mr. Cooper. I didn't yell, I didn't make a single sound. I just stared up at Mr. Cooper and walked back to my seat.

50

Notes:

Chapter 8: Ghetto Land

Chapter 8
Ghetto Land

At first I thought my school was just a ghetto school! Then I realized it's just some of the kids in it, or just the things some of the kids do. So here's a chapter on some of my classmates' ghetto moments. Everyone on board for ghetto landopolis.

Recently, my friend, Trish...

Trish: class rebel, funny, cool friend, crazy, curses, wrote a story for her own amusement. The story was called Ghetto Cinderella. It was hysterical! It was basically a remake of the original Cinderella, but things like the conflict between Cinderella and her stepsisters were more extreme. For example, when the family got an invitation to the prince's ball, and they tried to make Cinderella stay home...she ended up cursing out her sisters, saying things like "F you," you "B." Trish was confident about her story and it was funny. Then of course Mr. Cooper came over and interrupted us once again, like how he always does. The buzzkill.

Example 2:

Next, another ghetto moment would be caused by Tea. Tea does A LOT of ghetto things. She even talks in a ghetto way. Alright, so I'm sure we've all had that day when we're rushing to get to school or perhaps even a ghetto moment, yet we still want to eat something...we grab something small and leave. At my school, mainly in the morning, I'm used to kids coming in with white containers filled with fries and that's because there is a corner store that sells fries. They're located literally right next to my school.

Store → House → School

But, apparently, those options weren't noticed by Tea. Now, I know fries aren't the best eating choice for breakfast, but I feel what Tea did was just so ghetto. She walked into the classroom during homeroom eating a box of cereal. The box was in one hand and the other hand was being used to scoop out the cereal. Then she'd cram the cereal in to her mouth.

Mia and I were sitting together and we asked why Tea had to bring the ENTIRE box of cereal?!? She answered us by talking with a mouth full of Cocoa Pebbles and moving her hand in the air, in a motion that makes it look like she's trying to grab something.

Those were two of my classmates' ghetto moments.
#keepitclassyandtrashy

Notes:

_____

_____

_____

_____

_____

_____

_____

_____

Chapter 9: Last Day at Last

Chapter 9

Last Day at Last

Everything seemed to be going swiftly and as decent as it can get, and before any of us knew it was the last day of school. Now it wasn't announced on the previous school day that we could dress down, in other words, not wear our uniforms. But, it was the last day of school and no one really cared. Honestly, I didn't either.

I wore denim washed high-waisted jeans, a white fringe T-shirt with graphic lips, pink Essynce Couture lipstick, and to top it off...I put my hair in a bun. Oh! Let's also not forget my multi colored Adidas. With a quick look in the mirror, I was satisfied.

On my way to school, I had butterflies. I was a bit nervous that I'd be one of only a few who dressed down. I didn't want to embarrass myself. But, all that doubt went away as soon as my mom pulled up to the school. 95% of the school was dressed down. After a wave of relief washed over me, I made my way into the building.

In Mr. Cooper's class, he gave us some news. Some of us were shocked and others expected it. I felt both. Mr. Cooper told us that he'd been offered a few different jobs from a few different schools. He was no longer going to be a teacher in our school. To tell you the truth, I think that was the best decision he made. Mr. Cooper was unfortunately far from ready to handle our middle school chronicles and A LOT of people knew that.

Surprisingly, my friends and I really didn't talk about it that much. Then again, we weren't really surprised. Adios Mr. Cooper, you had a good amount of knowledge in Math in you...Not!

The rest of the day was pretty awesome. We did word searches and colored while hanging out with our friends in every class. When the bell rang signaling five minutes till the end of the day, my friends and I couldn't stop smiling. I bet you know the feeling, don't you?

I had come up with the idea that once the final bell rang, we all play a particular song that seemed to fit the moment. Ten seconds were left till the bell rang and everyone was counting down.

Ring! Ring! Ring!

There it was…all of my friends and I clicked play and the songs seemed to boost our new adrenaline rush. Guess what song we listened to?

Turn...

Down...

For...

What...

Once we entered the hall heading towards our doors of freedom, everyone started screaming with excitement. Summer here we come!!! The weather was awesome outside and some of us started saying bye to one another. I took a few selfies with my friends and then I was off to Freedom, Warmth, and Summer.

Notes:

_____

_____

_____

_____

_____

_____

_____

_____

_____

Chapter 10: 6th Grade Middle School Chronicles

Chapter 10

6th Grade Middle School Chronicles

To sum it all up, 6th grade was a bunch of things for me:

- **Fun**
- **Annoying**
- **Weird**
- **Different**

But, it's an experience I can promise I definitely won't forget. In conclusion, 6th grade was a heck of a year, and it proved that no one is perfect. Also, it showed me that you don't always need a magical wardrobe that can put you in an alternate universe to make your own little chronicle. School is an adventure itself and that's what I learned in my 6th Grade Middle School Chronicles.

"What you see and hear depends a good deal on where you are standing: it also depends on what sort of person you are."

The Chronicles of Narnia

THE END...for now because after these two months of freedom, we're all going to be forced against our will to come back to prison...Uh, I mean school. I think

---

I went around asking multiple 6th Graders in my school to write down an embarrassing moment they've had this year. At first they were reluctant which is understandable, but once I told them their names would be anonymous they agreed. They knew exactly what I was going to do with these stories and I thought that was AWESOME. To be able to get all these stories from the "populars" and "misfits," these embarrassments proved that we aren't a "popular" "misfit" or "athlete" or whatever label of judgment this society seems to come up with next. We are all HUMANS!!! Perfectly imperfect humans and I'm okay with that. After all, it's not like I really have a choice, just kidding...maybe.

Notes:

_____

_____

_____

_____

_____

_____

_____

_____

_____

THE END

6th Grade Middle School Chronicles

Where NO Secrets Are Kept

Written by

Essynce E. Moore

The Fashionista

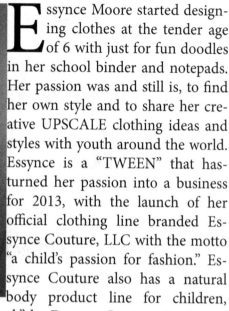

Essynce Moore started designing clothes at the tender age of 6 with just for fun doodles in her school binder and notepads. Her passion was and still is, to find her own style and to share her creative UPSCALE clothing ideas and styles with youth around the world. Essynce is a "TWEEN" that has turned her passion into a business for 2013, with the launch of her official clothing line branded Essynce Couture, LLC with the motto "a child's passion for fashion." Essynce Couture also has a natural body product line for children, tweens, and teens labeled "Wynk" by Essynce Couture. Essynce is an entrepreneur, children's stylist, child's fashion designer, actress, "local" celebrity, motivational speaker, author, and fashionista that brings a positive vibe to her peers and others. She's been in numerous fashion shows, pageants, and karate tournaments. She has SHOWCASED at both NY Fashion Weeks and Atlanta Kids Fashion Week while also ripping the runway. In addition, in 2014 she was interviewed and featured on NBC (Channel 4 News), Jeff Foxx of WBLS FM, BuzzFeed, Yahoo, Verizon Fios Channel 1 News, NBC Channel 4 News, she was awarded "2014 Young Emerging Leader" by Alpha Kappa Alpha, she's been featured in the 2013 TIME for Kids Magazine, Honored 2013 Entrepreneur of the Year by the Vashti School for Future Leaders, she's been seen on the Uncle Majic Commercial (BET, VH1, Channel 11, etc), HBO (Bored to Death), and has involved herself with a host of other events and projects.

Essynce is also a member of the New York Youth Chamber of Commerce (NYYCC).

This young **"phenomenon"** is BUZZING and she can't wait to see children wearing her Essynce Couture brand all around the world.

The Essynce Couture Brand

What makes us unique?!? Essynce Couture, LLC is one of the 1st children's clothing lines designed by a child with "education" in mind. We focus on styling our clothes to compliment all sizes, races, and colors of all children around the world. In addition, we offer great incentives through our Essynce Couture membership program to the children who support Essynce Couture, LLC by allowing them the opportunity to show and prove. They can upload either their report cards, certificates, awards or any other form of achievement(s) to one of the Essynce Couture social networks (instagram, twitter, or facebook) and may be selected to be rewarded by Essynce Couture, LLC incentives. This will encourage children to continue to do well in school and remind them that education is very important, rewarding, stylish, and can be fun!

www.essyncecouture.com

These are the EMBARRASEMENTS of my fellow 6th graders and maybe sometime in the future they'll tell you "WHO" anonymous really is.

Xoxo,

Essynce

Anonymous Embarrasements

1. When I got caught passing notes to someone in class and I bet the teacher read it.

2. When me and this boy got caught kissing.

3. When I got faded in a dance battle.

4. When I was on this boy and I got caught by one of the teachers.

5. I slipped outside when it was raining in front of people.

6. A couple of days ago I ripped my pants from the front to the back and kids from school saw.

7. Falling in the mud while walking to school and my sister and kids from school saw; my uniform was a mess.

8. When I got yelled at by my reading teacher for talking.

9. Almost fell on the floor while everybody was there.

Anonymous Embarrasements Continued

10. Once I slipped/fell in front of my crush.

11. I got my pants pulled all the way down by someone and they saw my green and black boxers.

12. Once my friend yelled my crush's name in front of everybody.

13. Almost fell down the steps and people was laughing.

14. Almost fell while running to class.

15. I got yelled at by a teacher for making faces in class.

16. I got caught kissing this boy in the hallway.

17. The time I went to gym without a bra.

18. I slipped on ice outside in front of everybody.

My personal embarrassment:

19. Once I entered the school building, heading towards where everybody else was waiting for their teachers. I sat next to my friends in the auditorium and a 8th grader came up to me and she whispered to me that a bra, which happened to be mine from home, was dangling off the side of my book bag. Almost all the 6th, 7th, and 8th graders saw my bra hanging off my book bag.

~ Essynce Moore

Don't be shy, write down your embarrassing moment(s) in one of our "notes" section. We've all had them.

Notes:

_____

_____

_____

_____

_____

_____

_____

_____

_____

Essynce E. Moore